FIESTAS

Diwali

Nancy Dickmann

Heinemann Library
Chicago, Illinois

www.heinemannraintree.com

Visit our website to find out more information about Heinemann-Raintree books.

To order:

☎ Phone 888-454-2279

🖥 Visit www.heinemannraintree.com to browse our catalog and order online.

Edited by Sian Smith, Nancy Dickmann, and Rebecca Rissman
Designed by Steve Mead
Picture research by Elizabeth Alexander
Production by Victoria Fitzgerald
Originated by Capstone Global Library Ltd
Printed and bound in China by South China Printing Company Ltd
Translation into Spanish by DoubleOPublishing Services

The content consultant was Richard Aubrey. Richard is a teacher of Religious Education with a particular interest in Philosophy for Children.

14 13 12 11 10
10 9 8 7 6 5 4 3 2 1

Library of Congress Cataloging-in-Publication Data

Dickmann, Nancy.
 Diwali / Nancy Dickmann.
  p. cm.—(Fiestas)
 Includes bibliographical references and index.
 ISBN 978-1-4329-5381-2 (hc)—ISBN 978-1-4329-5400-0 (pb)
1. Divali—Juvenile literature. I. Title.
 BL1239.82.D58D53 2011b
 294.5'36—dc22   2010034152

Acknowledgments

We would like to thank the following for permission to reproduce photographs: Alamy pp. **7** (© discpicture), **8** (© Tim Gainey), **9** (© Mary Evans Picture Library), **16** (© Visage), **19**, **23 bottom** (© Peter Brown), **20**, **23 top** (© Art Directors & TRIP), **21** (© Louise Batalla Duran); Corbis pp. **10** (© Historical Picture Archive), **17** (© Mark Bryan Makela); Getty Images pp. **6**, **23 bottom** (Narinder Nanu/AFP), **14** (Asif Hassan/AFP); Photolibrary pp. **4** (India Picture), **5**, **23 top** (Mohammed Ansar/Imagestate), **11**, **12**, **15** (Photos India), **13** (Alex Mares-Manton/Asia Images); Shutterstock pp. **18** (© jamalludin), **22 top left** (© Ronald Chung), **22 top right** (© Nir Levy), **22 bottom left** (© Stephane Breton), **22 bottom right** (© Mahantesh C Morabad).

Front cover photograph of traditional pooja thali reproduced with permission of Photolibrary (Hemant Mehta/India Picture RF). Back cover photograph reproduced with permission of Photolibrary (Photos India).

We would like to thank Diana Bentley, Dee Reid, Nancy Harris, and Richard Aubrey for their invaluable help in the preparation of this book.

Every effort has been made to contact copyright holders of any material reproduced in this book. Any omissions will be rectified in subsequent printings if notice is given to the publisher.

Contenido

¿Qué es una fiesta?

Una fiesta es una ocasión en que las personas se reúnen para celebrar.

Los hindúes celebran el Diwali
en otoño.

Los sijes también celebran el Diwali.

vela del Diwali

El Diwali se conoce como el Festival de las luces. Se encienden velas especiales.

La historia del Diwali

Rama

Sita

Hace mucho tiempo, vivió un príncipe llamado Rama. Tenía una esposa llamada Sita.

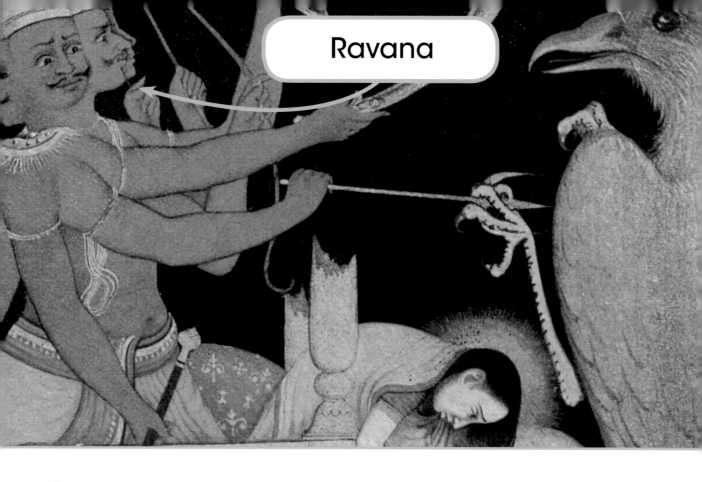

Sita fue raptada por un malvado rey llamado Ravana.

Rama venció a Ravana en una batalla.
Entonces Sita pudo regresar a casa.

La gente encendió velas para mostrarles a Rama y a Sita el camino a casa.

Celebrar el Diwali actualmente

En Diwali, las personas recuerdan la historia de Rama y Sita.

Algunas personas piensan en otras historias sobre el triunfo del bien sobre el mal.

vela del Diwali

Las personas encienden velas en
sus casas.

Hacen dibujos en el umbral de sus casas.

Se entregan tarjetas y regalos.

Bailan y tocan música.

Miran los fuegos artificiales.

mandir

Van al mandir.

Le dan la bienvenida a Lakshmi.

Esperan que les traiga buena suerte para el próximo año.

Buscar y ver

vela del Diwali

fuegos artificiales

Lakshmi

dibujos

¿Has visto estas cosas? Hacen que las personas piensen en el Diwali.

Glosario ilustrado

 **hindúes** personas que siguen las enseñanzas de la religión del hinduismo

 **Lakshmi** diosa hindú de la riqueza y la buena suerte

 **mandir** edificio donde los hindúes practican sus ceremonias religiosas

 **sijes** personas que creen en las enseñanzas de los gurús. Los gurús fueron importantes hombres santos de la India.

23

Índice

Nota a padres y maestros

Antes de leer

Pregunte a los niños si saben qué son las fiestas. ¿Pueden nombrar algunas fiestas que celebren con sus familias? Comente la diferencia entre las fiestas comunes y las fiestas religiosas. Explique que el Diwali es una fiesta que celebran los hindúes, quienes siguen la religión del hinduismo, y los sijes, quienes siguen la religión del sijismo. El Diwali a veces se escribe con "v", pero ambas palabras se refieren a la misma fiesta. El Diwali se llama el Festival de las luces.

Después de leer

• Hable sobre las velas del Diwali y las cosas que puede representar la luz, como la bondad, la esperanza y la sabiduría. Explique a los niños que otras religiones también usan la luz como símbolo, como en la fiesta judía de Janucá. Muéstreles fotos de velas del Diwali y ayúdelos a diseñar su propia vela.

• Hable del Diwali como un momento de optimismo o esperanza y de nuevos comienzos. Comente que esto se corresponde con las actividades tradicionales del Diwali, como limpiar las casas, sembrar cultivos o vestirse con ropas nuevas. Pida a los niños que piensen en maneras en que podrían tener un "nuevo comienzo". Podría sugerir algunas ideas, como resolver las diferencias con los amigos, comenzar un nuevo proyecto o limpiar la habitación.